Braille

Rainbow

poems

Mike
Barnes

BIBLIOASIS

WINDSOR, ONTARIO

FIRST EDITION

Library and Archives Canada Cataloguing in Publication

Barnes, Mike, 1955-, author
      Braille rainbow / Mike Barnes.
Poems.

Issued in print and electronic formats.
ISBN 978-1-77196-221-6 (softcover).--ISBN 978-1-77196-222-3 (ebook)

      I. Title.

PS8553.A7633B73 2019   C811'.54   C2018-904428-4
                                                 C2018-904429-2

Edited by Zachariah Wells
Copy-edited by Emily Donaldson
Typeset and designed by Chris Andrechek

Published with the generous assistance of the Canada Council for the Arts, which last year invested $153 million to bring the arts to Canadians throughout the country, and the financial support of the Government of Canada. Biblioasis also acknowledges the support of the Ontario Arts Council (OAC), an agency of the Government of Ontario, which last year funded 1,709 individual artists and 1,078 organizations in 204 communities across Ontario, for a total of $52.1 million, and the contribution of the Government of Ontario through the Ontario Book Publishing Tax Credit and the Ontario Media Development Corporation.

PRINTED AND BOUND IN CANADA

Contents

Knives in High Places

Pry Bars

Braille Rainbow

Admission Suite

Admission Suite

The thirteen poems that follow were written in the days just before, and just after, I was admitted to St. Joseph's Hospital, Hamilton, in November 1977, diagnosed with acute schizophrenia. (When I re-entered psychiatric treatment in 1990, after more than a decade avoiding it, I was told that the initial diagnosis had been incorrect, that instead I had bipolar disorder.) After this flurry of poems, the Red Book—a thick hardbound book with unlined pages and a pebbly red cover, which I had been rapidly filling with writing and drawings—went blank white. It stayed that way. I was, I'm told, completely catatonic for a time and then intermittently so. I have relatively few, and very fragmented, memories of the eighteen months that followed. I didn't resume writing until 1979, some weeks after my discharge. I used a new notebook.

As a document from that time, the poems are presented here unrevised; in a few cases I can recall, or reconstruct, the exact circumstances of their composition. The poem "fruit bat," appropriately in the middle of the sequence, was written while I rode the bus from Toronto to Hamilton to be admitted after doctors at North York General had stitched up the deep lacerations I had made in my abdomen—my "self-Caesarean"—and elsewhere on my body. It is a wonder to me that I wrote the six poems after it, given the regimen of heavy tranquilizers I was started on immediately. But ingrained habits die hard, and for a short time drug uptake did battle with a creative outpouring. It was after I'd showed these poems to staff, I'm also told, that *hebephrenia*—betokening radical incoherence, a childish beyond-reachness—became a stable entry on my chart.

11

a madman cut and blessed the air
and read each day from a book of prayer

when he reached the last page out he fled
"you must write another book" it said

what if a man

what if a man should wake one morning
with white and trembling hands
his hair composed
(literally) of vanishing filaments
and his bones
rattling—rhythm
of seeds in a gourd

and what if this same man
feeling as angry
but also as carefree and sequent
as an acorn
dropped from a branch

should see his wife
standing in the doorway
and think only

of poppy seeds, scattering

would not this man soon give signs
he had developed
unholy loves and fears

self-hate

cast your prejudicial eye
into the sea. as it falls
mumble something bitterly
about an eyepiece that floats.

rescue attempt

i had an aunt with a heart condition
who lived in Saint John's.
so i took the bus to see her
but the driver talked so much about his daughter

living in sin
that we both decided to go there
and bring her back instead.
i had no clear idea how to get there

and he only knew it was a harrowing place
full of inversions.
so we asked a boy with a chestnut on a string
who was playing

but he cracked me on the head with the chestnut
and said nothing.
i asked the driver if this was rude
and he agreed to help me whip him.

afterwards he asked me if i was hungry
and i said yes.
so we flayed a cucumber in the striped sun
and ate it.

new friends

      vase, milk,
      salt,
the coat in the hall;
      perfunc

      tory rows
of wine bottles: glass skins
      emptied
      by the

slender meshing of friends.
      now: cotton
      shirts, books,
pictures and windows: ancillary friends.

      after twenty
      years, a
tide has gone out. i am alone:
a delicate saw of bone under a bone sky.

fishcleaning

i gut the slim forms you pass
me in silence:
> bass
> perch
> bullhead (black
> & pin-eyed)

puckish sunfish
bleeding a red dawn

pike. pike last. slashes
around the gills, and the river boa
shivers. he vomits up a minnow
and the little corn-coloured whelp
lies curled, inside the
scythe teeth.

as the guts are wrenched free and flung away
the pike's jaw sags.

the wind
> scoots up a windstorm of scales.
> > > the minnow

falls into the grass.

fruit bat

you called me mad: when i hung upsidedown in a fruit
                                 tree whistling for fruit

you called me mad: when winter came and i still
                                 hung black and folded

you called me mad: when the wind shrieked and my wings
                                 beat against my body for warmth

you called me mad: when springsummerfall
                                 the black pendant hung

you called me mad: when i starved but couldn't leave
                                 and sharp teeth gnawed my own belly

nightmare

itches

the body sends its prickling missive
warning of the skin-web and the filth of the spider
sitting hairy-legged where the hair was
holding the head rigid preparing to suck
the mouth an incredible jelly-bag of filth

SHAKE IT SHAKE IT SHAKE IT smear it into the pillow
churn its boneless malevolence into pulp
and fall back gasping into sleep

WAKE what seems seconds later to a new battle
a struggling of planes of sheet skin and darkness
a horrible dance of angles
the greatest most noiseless intersections clanging like snow

hairball life drops suddenly and runs scuttling
across the room holding his ears
in fear in anger he begins to eat
he eats the furniture the wall he eats bill
sleeping next to me he eats all
he eats the meat hunched down over darkness
right down to the bone of light
a handsome gleaming bone of rapidly accumulating flesh

so exhausted i lay my head next
to this the day's expanding muzzle
and am soon swallowed whole into sleep

a paltry wakefulness

i wake on a psychiatric ward
amazed to notice my bottom becoming
soft, less definitely globed
sloping as stately as a woman's

        —hospital "food"!

visitors, visitations—
violet cauliflowered exhalations of pipe smoke

there is a film in front of my eyes
coming from my eyes
as if a grasshopper had attached to those skeins
and hopped away erratically
randomly unravelling them

(these are deep soft wounds)

i feel like thin metal
twisted under Giacometti's fingers
to a stalk of fibrous leaning in space

but the bitterest irony is the self
imitating itself at every level
until even emptiness fails to inhabit

fails to be more real
than a shard of slivered light
thrown from the throat

to be caught by the eyes and cloned into space

failed inventory

the chair chaired the meeting

the pen penned the minutes
the ball balled the minutes into time

the pattern patterned itself
the colour coloured the pattern
the light lighted the colour

the colour coloured the light
the house housed secrets
the earth unearthed them
the space spaced the house from the earth

the fish fished in the river
the sand sanded down the rock
the rock rocked underneath
the I—————

what does it do? i cried to the
chair pen ball pattern colour light
colour house earth space fish sand rock I

but none of them could stop what they were doing to answer
and the I the I the I the I

eyed everything nervously

the 1st order of genius

the 1st order of genius can extract huge sums with a flourish

the 2nd order wanders through a labyrinth in his nightshirt
        carrying a candle

the 3rd order is a more servile courtier. he reads at home to his kids
        while golden hooves flash in his head

the 4th order has a tiered trachea, able to swallow anything
        he is called cudbag, but he eats adjectives

the 5th order appears at the corner of your vision and walks
        across it, a nimble and professional motion

the 6th order says cuntshitprick how i hate to get up in the
        morning and falls dead

there are many more orders of genius. while still
a gambolling freeloader in my mother's womb, i counted
millions of them. others have documented them more thoroughly
        than i

listen paper

don't call me honest. just flash the blade
that fetches an exact smear.

don't set me up either as wise: my head is only my
neck looking in one direction.

paperglass scissorsstone, i love all sided things:
if i thought truth was round shit
i would sew up my asshole
and take to painting like a cubist.

i admit: what is clear
i encase in clear amber, hardening the illusion.

scissors stone, love is good. perhaps
because the cunt is warm and the cock is long
enough. goodday.

fish live in the toilet,
they come up to see me.
fish live in the toilet,
how they flash merrily!

Day Pass

The Check-Out King

He died in his mid-twenties
(nobody seemed to know what of),
got himself safely underground
before the rest of us had our first cancer scare.
He was always slipping past the lens,
over at the cropped edge of the class picture
or dead centre in an egg of glare.
He might be at the vortex of a scrum or rumble
or flopped down in the field beyond the goal,
oblivious to calls for his return, watching
(perhaps) an ant traverse a blade of grass.
In those days no work meant you failed.
"Have you finished, Earl?" the teacher
asked when his head sank onto his arms.
"No." "Have you started?" "No."
Everyone, even she, laughed. Everyone
except Earl. He rode out humour
the way a pine tree rides out rain.
A cipher makes a tricky victim:
he may become a black hole or a mirror.
Our bully picked him out only when
he'd run through everyone else at least twice.
Earl didn't confront, didn't retreat.
He stood there and one punch knocked him flat.
He lay a while with his face to the sky
(so long that some of us
looked up too—just blue and fluffy clouds)

and then got up and walked away
toward wherever he lived, getting
slowly small, every few steps
bringing a hand to his face and
flinging a ribbon of blood at the dust.

Bill Had

Two deaf parents who taught him sign language,
which he forgot after they died.
Next to mine, the best beat-up old denim jacket
in the crew.
Small hands for such a big man.
Thick dark hair, hazel eyes, and the handsomest
face I've seen outside of Hollywood.
A talent for mimicry.
An irritating habit of taking things too far.
An endearing one of apologizing when he did.
Small learning and large curiosity.
A pretty short attention span.
An unshakeable belief that women ejaculated
when they came.
Many girlfriends.
Dozens of friends, including ex-girlfriends.
A part-time DJ job where he met many of his friends
and girlfriends and scored high-quality drugs.
Inoperable colon cancer at age 28.
A cop costume so good it almost got him beaten up
by Hallowe'en partiers who had flushed their dope
until he shared out his own, which was better.
A filthy apartment piled with pizza boxes.
A grin no one could resist.
Nimble feet, with which he performed amusing untrained
tap, soft shoe, and jig.
Zero ambition.

Occasional mean moods but no cruel bone in his body.
A Jimmy Cagney routine in which while singing "Yankee
Doodle Dandy" he ran at a wall and up it and back-
flipped off of it, landing on his feet,
which never should have worked because Cagney
was a shrimp and Bill was fullback-sized
but I saw it, many times, from 1981 to 1985,
during the long afternoons when the galleries
were empty.

My Bosses

Come quitting time, they frowned, muttered, sighed;
glared, cursed my timing; one even cried.
Young Word-to-the-Wise prophesied dark days.
All sang of my worth. None offered a raise.

Never the Twain

The burghers look insane to me,
with their kids and pups, their SUVs;
I'm sure I look the same to them—
parked on a side street, chewing a pen.

Bliss

Wouldn't it be bliss to shove the dayjob
and just focus totally on writing?!!

Topics I've discussed with my students this week:

When and why and how to sit
still.
Reasons to wash your hands
after using the toilet.
The Great Oxidation Event.
Since anaerobic bacteria like awful places and
excrete oxygen, why we don't send
them to other planets to build atmospheres
for us.
What chickens see when they look at us.
Waiting for Godot. Why nothing keeps happening.
If nerve impulses are electro-chemical why
not construct nerve-pack generators.
What it means to say *People should be treated*
as ends not means.
Making a Rainbow Loom bookmark.
How not to fear death without God
or an afterlife.
Why *manga* characters, baby animals and super-
models have big eyes.
Jane Eyre's *I must begin a new*
existence amongst strange faces and strange scenes.

The meaning of *disdain*. *Gastroenterologist*. *Psyche*.
Factors affecting radicalization in British prisons.
Narrative criticisms of *Alice's Adventures in Wonderland*.
The need to keep clean so someone will love you.
Hew versus *hue*.
Being less original than your sister.

Remedies

For mosquitoes, repellent. For chest
colds, steam. For anger, time. For robbers, locks.
Against self-pity, strongest of pests?
Nothing for that but the final box.

Crosstown

Bell-crack cold a month now with no sign of snow.
Bushy squirrels mating in spider branches bare

as nails. Corpses arrive in crystal dawns:
slumped in a bus shelter, stretched out in a truck, curled

beneath charred junk in a vacant house set blazing.
Crosstown digging continues. Hardhats yellow and blue,

orange vests chirp a crayoned spring. Chipped manhole
covers glint beside access shafts steaming black.

Secure Ward

code

Can I come down
with you? No not this
time I'm afraid. *Not*

on this elevator? No not
this one. I'm sorry. Maybe the next.

2015

Why won't they let me see
my parents? Can you tell me that at least?

Your parents passed away a long
time ago. Your dad in 1963, Grandma in 1981.

Small tears brighten old eyes, find paths
down wrinkled cheeks. Nibbles of cupcake,

sips of lemon tea. *No. It's*
been a few days but they still come around.

Watch

Unzipped from dark
it is seven minutes slow,
one second lost

for each day off your wrist.
I hesitate, then cut
the plastic tag, your name

in a stranger's hand.
On my wrist the metal
cool. Finding warmth, it tingles.

The Men

Thick limbs glimpsed through steam, dangling
slab-muscled bodies so unlike your own, white
as the birch logs they, laughing, send you outside,
naked and important in the chill dusk, to poke
through a hole in the hut's burning belly, beneath
orange-gilled rocks. Pink-slatted too, those
great flanks, welted as if branded or flailed, pink
as woodland flowers you may have glimpsed, pink
as women's parts you haven't dreamed of yet.
Lake Nipissing, when you run with them whooping
into it, feels—*just cool*. Start of May. Ice ten
days out. Sauna is that strong a sorcerer. Keeping the
black lake back, then letting it creep in, and in, until,
a long half-minute, ice-jar shock makes you splash
and holler and run howling up the snow-striped mud
slope to dipper and steam, radiant rock cradle.

Dreams so single then: to play as utility forward
on the Montreal Canadiens' fourth line. To kiss
Kathy Lawrence. The trick with dreams, you sense
without thinking, is to span their distance from
reality, render the fuse-chopped gap crossable. But
life more mountain-strange than dreams, more
chock and various its constant drops and vistas.
Those men, one my father, both gone now. And
yet as they live in the sweating mist, young enough
to be my sons, though I have had no children.

Dreams, shy deer, pick unseen places in the woods
to curl upon themselves and join soft dark. After
ransack years, skirting death upon a narrow
wobbly beam, you become an ink man, poised to
spot the drop where steam and ice-water kiss.

Bumble Bounce Rag

One bee's
weight makes
the sprig
of goldenrod

dance.

Knives in High Places

Summer Suicides

How many kids have you seen, little ones,
who don't like to swim? Expats from the womb,
unless held back by fear or mother's arms,
they gambol again in grace-giving fluid,
spin fast bubbling somersaults.
At verge of grass, safe from splashing's range,
the amnio-amnesiac rest their spotted limbs,
watch heavy-lidded, with fond thin smiles.
The middle is a slippery, stuff-strewn zone
of psychic halflings: beached uncertainly,
sun-struck, cold, lithe-torpid and fat-spry,
they take quick lurching plunges to cool off,
chase a better body, bob up goggle-eyed,
then kick once and glide down to weed-columned halls.

Knives in High Places

What were you thinking? I don't say *you of all people*,
since anyone much past diapers should know blades
and top cupboards don't mix. And balanced on a plate?
What, so you could slice and nibble in ten seconds less?
Fate was civil. Your scar will give your glance new depth
and serve as a reminder, though why you'd need one—
Surely you recall some diagram of The Eye
or those peeled grapes that made us gasp on Hallowe'en.

Absentia

You planted the bomb that made a fuse
of her otherwise ribboned, striving days;
and loosed strange worms to churn into sand
her carefully cultivated land;
and blackened her memory with chars and twists
I have longed to visit upon you with fists—
except you absconded long ago,
taking all that she knew, leaving all that she knows.

"I have gained a strange disease"

On lilac-coloured paper
that has dried and tears crisply—
who were you that wrote these lines?

Where do you make your home now, and with whom?

Drinking Frappuccinos on a Dementia Ward

At last, the night-mind's unconsoled colic
—bleak lashing tears, fumblings in shredded
junk—gives way to day's sweet milk you
once brought me, need before word, word
before names, a world certified by just
this warmth, soft touch, familiar smells.

There are holes in your head, there are holes
in mine as well. I don't speak carelessly—
How could I in this place made only of
particulars: one bed, one bureau, two scuffed
chairs. A tiny plastic dog that was the year's best gift.

But heart is not a hole. In its dark, thick
wild shoots and rustlings, swarms of succulent
tiny tadpoles huddling in mud-rut puddles.
Deep earth hum of sitting quiet together.

This peace we sit in, sipping, being beyond
names, is beyond time as well, a thousand
day-nights passing exactly the same:
sun coming up, sun climbing a pale blue hill, sun
going down. Milk of moon and cloud changing places.

Pine trees are brushes
while their own hair grows;
dead, they are combs
broken bald in the snow.

August 15 2012

The world is small
and stretched tight like a drum

Everywhere I go
I hear your quiet footsteps beside me

Who has not seen
the glow of loved ones
vanish, never to return?

Who has not seen
each night the pitted moon
rise here, rise there?

Timeless

Today the clock unmade itself,
its coiled bright springs
laid down in blackness on the snow;

a sky above so bluely vast
the eyes in sidelong gulps must drink it in.
Such a pouring of to do, to wait—

all hurry gone. If but tomorrow
could be so redeemed, all
yesterday allow its ticking, its alarms.

March Squirrel

Wedged
blackly in
branches encased

in clear unbroken cold,
nothing in your paws
to peel or rotate,

your jaws gnaw
on hard, budless bark.
Winters

all have ends
save one. You and I,
can we mine null hours

to find ice flowering?

Mer Verse

Schooled I could not leave this element,
I tried to rise, and tried to rise,
and would not sink, and would not sink,
and, wave by wave, I breathed the peace was sent.

Our Ararat

What use a rainbow not in braille,
tidings other than the touch of feathers,
leaf's cool caress, hard prod of bill,
to gazes penned and floated beyond prayer?

We Are Here

Are you there, Richard—
painting in appalled tints
your drenched father's blood,
unseen by anyone
until the master stroke falls?

> From Broadmoor, faintly:
> *I am here.*

Are you there, William—
singing your brother's soul to heaven
three days straight
as angels in the frosty hawthorn
applaud your feat?

> *The Devil's Deny*
> *is His greatest Lie:*
> *Yes, I am Here!*

Are you there, Yayoi—
wise chooser of asylum,
elective permanent retreat
where the feverish swarming dots
surge undefiled in fiber?

> From a rice-paper plane:
> *I am here*
> *I am here.*

Are you there, Xu Wei,
Vincent, are you there—
airless marauders of pearl
from shells of glutinous striving
for ocean's moment?

> From a bower of grapes
> and unlaced boots:
> *Yes, we are here.*

Are you there, Judy—
daubing holy rape
upon tissues of nightgown
by bedsides in the undark ward
where your smashed face shines?

> In murmur tinier than a fly's:
> *I am...here.*

Are you there—
my years and heroes,
avatars of shatter and rebar,
shard reconveners,
my undead selves your peers?

> Firmly, through the collapsed
> masonry, rubble's echo climbs:
> *We are here. We are here.*

Pry Bars

Hummingbird

Smashed in flight
against the window glass,
it has fallen to this
improbable perch, a
seated man's shoulder.

His Rushmore profile
gapes across three inches
at the iridescent head
and pipe-bowl body
anchored on thread feet
stitched to denim.

Well may these small
wings folded flat
resume their blur
and lift him
to his feet again.

Cell Inventory

The crack in my wall
    is a river,
forking its way through the desert.
The ant is a lion
    pacing by the river.

And the shadow, shapeless,
that darkens river and lion?

And the light, invisible,
that shows me where I live?

Pry Bars

I'm trying to learn to trust myself.
> *Why, are you trustworthy?*

It lacks depth.
> *Worse, it lacks surface.*

I control my destiny.
> *Is it that small?*

Nothing can be done.
> *Everything may be tried.*

Ikebana

Artfully impaled
in a shallow, weighted bowl

by one who understands
and can balance

purples, greens and creams
the iris and the lily

are not less lovely
and consolingly

themselves, rooted
in a soil of needles

On Coming into Possession of a Diary

The giant cast no shadow as he walked.
Which made the things and people that he loved love him back,
knowing he could hurt them and would not.

No dubious darkness such as trailed their lives,
cross-hatching each bright gesture with its own undoing,
trailed his. What he did, he did entire:

Dug wild leeks and coaxed from stone a garden,
drank beer from a sweating glass in sunset-purpled air,
built a trim shed, fought enemies, kept friends.

Solid in life and solider in death,
he feared no discovery and so he was discovered,
sealed in secrecy even from himself.

But where will revelation make a home
when orphans charged with its keeping have learned to live outdoors?
The one sewn into his long-shucked shadow.
The other tending his elected sun...

Mysteries

Grey doors in a grey hall,
   behind one is home.

Dark jelly of a million frogs
   clustered on stone.

"Let's clear the air"

Since my views on the matter
didn't matter when they mattered,
when suffering was acute and might be spared—

Why would I rehearse them
with those absent till the hearse came?
A vacuum means there's no air to be cleared.

So Far

What was that insight
you delayed a few moments
setting down, thinking it
so precious it would keep
—now gone? Later, with
luck, it will turn up on
some window sill, April's
Easter treat hidden too well,
July's dark egg baking
behind a curtain, runny
brown stain still sweet if
a little queer, its sugars
eerie in collected coils,
sucked from its shiny foil
wrapper hazed with sun,
worn half on face and hands,
summer beyond the pane
faded in unfocused glare looking
with its secret gone
so far along, along.

Tangent: Lines by a Bed

Lees of loss, typhoon renewals—all mapped.
Can you tack into the strangeness that is sanity?

In. Out? Spirit bubble in your throat the whole
globe's turning. *Hold it, floating, a moment longer.*

Shadow is light's mute ecstasy.

Three Days Dry

Bigger and closer. Things jumping
to view in random zooms. My own
eyes lunging at me from mirrors. Looking
a little clearer (is this possible already?)
with more green mixed into the brown
than I remember. Effect of moss, rain-
washed, gleaming from old-growth hollows.

A space. Thin envelope of air, or
not air, around what I seem to be doing.
Like one of those clearings we kept
watch for while camping.
Silence. Not ringing yet but feeling it could.
That church-like sense, as we laid out our gear,
of a place set apart from the forest.

Cold Fireflies

Right-minded so far today
after three months of crazy—
what relief can compare?
It's too deep for joy. Too delicate.

Just now. Watch these specks
of snow, so tiny, so intermittent,
appear and disappear in the air,
jig this way and dance that, cold

fireflies, some finding their way
to the dark ground, where they melt.

Heart

Which is worse: self-
pity all say avoid, or
self-pitilessness? Burst
into shards again, why
not spare a moan for
loss, for creature pain,
even as you bend to
gather and glue,
gather and glue.
Heart so avid to mend
brokenness, glad spending
saving too, save a little
for the brokenness known
longest but not best.

Counsellors

"Try," said the sun
to the autumn tree,
and draped harvest warmth
on its withering.

    And nothing was changed
    in the tree's sinking.

"Try," said a brown-backed
bee in spring,
scrabbling to sip
from a threadbare bloom.

    And nothing was changed
    in the tree's slow ruin.

"Try," said the summertime
child who played,
climbing crooked limbs,
dreaming dappled shade.

    And nothing was changed
    and the child grew away.

"Don't try," said a star
a thousand years burst.
"My afterlife's gleam
ignites the frost."

  And nothing was changed
  by duration's boast.

"Don't try," said a root
in the secret soil.
"When green, you split rock.
Now lean with the gale."

  And nothing was changed
  and the tree toppled whole.

Braille Rainbow

Drowsing While Reading a Book of Chinese Poems

for Heather

Drowsing while reading a book
              of Chinese poems
I wake to see you again
on that long-ago April morning:
bent forward to support
the enormous pack
that carried your books and binders
              of drawings,
you trudged up the shoulder
of an ice-rutted road, in bouncing sunlight,
and when I slowed my car
              to greet you
you flashed, in quick succession,
a startled, green-gold stare,
a crooked grin, and then an awkward
              peace sign.

Nightfall

The two of us in a white boat,
casting contentedly, without hope
as dusk falls in the quiet bay.

In the mirror stillness
at end of day, or beginning of night,
we hear water

moving, trickling, somewhere near us.
Somewhere near us water is flowing
into, or going out of, this great river.

Now it is dark. We have stopped
fishing and are just sitting, listening
to the sound, a little louder now,

of a great bathtub draining, or filling, slowly.

He Who Stretches His Line

In 1551, aged eighty-one,
the painter Wen Zhengming
sketched eight views in ink
of the *Garden of the Inept Administrator*,
each one including a poem
of immaculate resignation
executed in flashing brush strokes:

...You must know that he who stretches his line,
Is not one who desires to catch fish.

Another Ming painter
of a little later, Xu Wei,
depicted grapes and melons and
pomegranates
in a style of inksplash freshness,
suffered severe mental breakdown,
killed his second wife, and
after getting out of jail
lived out his seventy-two years
in poverty, sickness, and solitude.

Neither man achieved his first ambition.
Wen failed the local
civil service exam ten times,
Xu got past the county
test and then failed at the provincial
level eight times in a row.

From the haze around these far-off
Chinese gentlemen
I seem to step out clearly:
hardly an inept administrator or
helpless vagrant, I am one whose early
promise was exploded by psychosis
—it is a time to speak unmistakably—
the decades since
a picking up and dropping again
of the pieces I could salvage
in a swamp between dread waters and dry land.

I am not quite at my wit's end.
But now neither time nor health is on my side.
Now I will need the good fortune
of long life
to even hope to sketch my vision,
to reach the white stone
and jade-like pool
where I may lower my dry line.

Morning Glories in a Planter Brought Indoors, November

Frail funnels of blue-
purple and pink-mauve,
autumn-watered hues of old
veins spread trembling
under a skin of mottled
green-brown leaves flattened
to glass. Unseen, unloved,
you gathered in night's crooked
elbow your terrible thinned
strength to face this grey
dawn backlit by shapeless
white, trickling and flaring
to animate a hand,
hand to make a
mouth. Mouth
saying *wait*. Saying
behold. Saying
kiss me.

The Skin of Things

Why did they tell me
(and I told myself)
that what I needed
must be hidden
deep

in a secret compartment
or treasure chest
only years of commitment
—work, books, cheques,
tears, vows, dearth—
could hope to unearth?

All wrong. Like an angel
harping at a grave
when it could just up
and fly. Because it's here
at the skin of things—
this skin, this this, this now—
the surface I've been
missing with my digging.

It's more obvious
than air. (Too obvious
to see.) What air
might surround or be
surrounded by
everywhere. And I
breathe it without breathing.

Lazy Song at Last

Write this on the breezes stirring
in this quiet, nameless spot where

woodland rock descends to wetlands.
Take the ambitions I've no use for

anymore, sail them on a maple key
down this trickle emptying the bog.

With luck they'll find the river I
hear faintly beyond the trees, maybe

reach Lake Huron before freeze-up.
But even if they stop at the next

windless inlet, snagged on some chance
tangle of debris, it's enough to watch

as they drift silently away, helped
by these straying breaths of pine.

East Window

Inching my chair
back to stay
in sun's slant path,

its February arc brisk
beyond this east
window. Frugal

as a basking lizard, I
finally run out of speckled
ledge, find myself

in cool shadow, beside
the Christmas cactus.
Flowering

again, it needs water.

Hold Hands

after Robert Fulghum

Hold hands, yes, when crossing busy streets,
on icy sidewalks, on slippery stairs,
hold hands when strolling in the park,
hold hands when walking to the convenience
store and back again. Hold hands if you feel like it.
Hold hands when receiving milk from another's body,
or offering it, or looking on as a not-so-innocent bystander.
Hold hands before you kiss,
hold hands after making love.
Hold hands like they do in the movies
(there's no need to be original),
hold hands when no one else is doing it
and when everyone in sight already is.
Hold hands with strangers,
not every chance you get but
more often than you do now.
Hold hands when getting good news
you can't believe, hold hands
when getting bad news you can.
Hold hands today, you'll thank yourself tomorrow
and—this part's magical—you'll thank yourself yesterday too.
Hold hands when you feel like it and sometimes when you
don't. Hold hands across a table in a restaurant
and in waiting rooms, and as the plane takes off
and lands. Hold hands when it's obviously
the right thing to do, and sometimes when it might be
the wrong thing—chance it then sometimes too.

Hold hands at your own times, for your own reasons.
Hold hands at home.
Hold hands with yourself (you don't need
to call it prayer though you're welcome to).
Hold hands when the lights go down
and when they come back up again.
Hold hands at awesome spectacles, hold hands
at ordinary ones, hold hands at famous fabulous
landmarks and famous boring ones.
Hold hands when you're least expected to
and also when you're most expected to
(this was said already but it's important).
Hold hands at places and events too numerous
to mention and easily imagined by anybody:
beaches, fireworks displays, off and on in
movies, your child's first recital, your child's
last recital, someone's graduation, entering or leaving a cemetery...
Hold hands soon after reading this poem.
Hold hands long after you've forgotten it.
Hold hands when one or both of you
is going into the dark, and hold hands when one
of you doesn't come back. Keep holding hands
a little longer when an official- or kind-sounding voice
tells you it's time to let go, because it
isn't quite. Not yet. Hold hands.

Happiness

Morning after another night of working
    late,
my eyes trace lines my mind's too tired
    to take in;
from beyond the glass a sparrow's cheep
    rings,
cheep cheep cheep—a new sound, though who knows
    when it began.
Dust motes tumble in a haze
    of autumn sunlight.
Soon, in rooms nearby, the neighbours
    will be rising.

Alive

Bright copper sparks from the sidewalk
in strong spring light. Peer down. Curved

copper back of a speck-sized bug, dome
of some microscopic faith—flaring, flaring.

Dogs' feet, people's feet, stroller wheels pass
heedlessly above. On it basks, a dot alive.

The Door

Standing on that road
outside Blaubeuren
            even the dust
shines & is white

staring with eyes
newly concentrated
at the wheatfield becoming

more than wheat, or
for the first time, wheat

a vibratory world
of timeless power, humming
molecular swarm
& awesome geometry

razor-sharp planes

            electric blue &
            liquid gold—

If I could see,
then, the battering years
ahead:

shocked, drugged, poor;
or just that one terrible
moment when I smashed
my head again & again
on the linoleum floor
to free it—

would I still stare
through this shimmering door

feeling myself enter?

Acknowledgements

"The Check-Out King," in a slightly different form, was published in *The New Quarterly*.

Thank you to my editor, Zach Wells, who encouraged me to include the "Admission Suite" poems and whose sharp ear and astute suggestions improved many of the others.

Thank you to the people of Biblioasis, for making such beautiful books and for making working on them such a joy: Chris Andrechek, Meghan Desjardins, Emily Donaldson, Casey Plett, and Vanessa Stauffer.

Thank you, first and last, to Dan Wells, for building this fine house and repeatedly welcoming me into it; for his tact, tenacity, intelligence, and generosity; especially, for his friendship through a baker's dozen of years.

This book is dedicated with love to Heather Simcoe.

About the Author

Mike Barnes is the author of eleven books of poetry, short fiction, novels, and memoir, including the novel *The Adjustment League*, *The Lily Pond: A Memoir of Madness, Mystery, Myth and Metamorphosis*, and, most recently, *Be With: Letters to a Caregiver*. He has won the Danuta Gleed Award and a National Magazine Awards Silver Medal for his short fiction, and the Edna Staebler Award for nonfiction. He lives in Toronto.